Stories From The Heart

carers' journeys at *Barefoot Birmingham Yoga*

Published in Great Britain in 2025
by Big White Shed, Morecambe, Lancashire
www.bigwhiteshed.co.uk
Printed and bound by Imprint Digital, Devon

ISBN 978-1-915021-44-1

Photogtaphs by members of the team and @Simon Crisp

A CIP catalogue record of this book is available from the British Library.

Foreword

In the pages that follow you will find a heartfelt collection of stories and poems penned by those who dedicate their lives to caring for relatives or friends in Birmingham, U.K. These family carers, who have found nourishment and community at *Barefoot*, navigate the complexities of compassion, resilience and sacrifice daily.

Their experiences, captured in this anthology, offer a glimpse into the profound and often challenging world of caregiving.

Each piece is a testament to the strength and humanity of carers. Through their words we are invited to walk alongside them, sharing in their moments of joy, sorrow, frustration and triumph. These narratives are not just reflections of their journeys but also a powerful reminder of the impact empathy and dedication can have on the lives of those they care for.

As you read through these stories and poems, you will encounter a diverse array of voices and perspectives. Some will make you smile, others may bring a tear to your eye, but all will leave you with a deeper understanding and appreciation for the vital role carers play in our society. Their experiences remind us of the importance of kindness, patience, and unwavering support in the face of adversity.

We hope this collection will inspire you, as it has inspired us to recognise and honour the incredible contributions of family carers everywhere. May their words resonate with you and encourage a greater sense of empathy and gratitude in your own life.

With heartfelt appreciation.

Contents

Introduction

Stories

Poems

Self-Care

Yoga & Wellbeing
barefoot
BIRMINGHAM

How The *Barefoot* Journey Began

After walking the streets of Birmingham and trawling the net for years, I knew immediately that *this was* the place. A slightly run-down solicitors office on a busy junction of Harborne High Street. It was empty, just a sea of thin blue carpet with a web of 1980's see-through offices and disconnected phone wires floating on top. Flimsy, half-glazed partitioned walls and life-draining strip lighting. It was horrible...and perfect! I knew right away that this that could become the wonderful community yoga and wellbeing sanctuary I'd been conjuring up. The beautiful light streaming through the windows made it easy to see how those temporary office walls could come tumbling down to create one big light-filled studio. A space to stretch, strengthen, smile and re-connect.

1,013 carers have been welcomed by us and found sanctuary at *Barefoot*

I remortgaged the family home, cut all my outgoings, begged and borrowed, applied for every grant going, and in September 2012 *Barefoot Birmingham Yoga Studio* was looking beautiful and open for business. My mission was simple: to offer a warm, welcoming gym alternative, where women (and men, if women-supporters) could come together to enjoy their bodies and de-clutter their minds through yoga, tea and chat. A place to escape the busyness of our always-on culture, and to learn simple ways to move, meditate and live more joyfully.

After an amazing opening week with busy classes and lots of interest, things suddenly went very quiet. That first year was extremely hard, with barely enough yogis to pay the bills. I was unsure of how long we could continue. But gradually yoga became mainstream; shop mannequins popping-up in yoga-wear, TV ads featuring couples in yoga poses, and suddenly we were no longer up against the old preconceptions of it being 'just for bendy types', or 'boring breathing', or 'just for women'. It was a relief.

439 carers are currently attending yoga and wellbeing sessions

Once on firmer ground, with over 20 studio classes a week, we set out to reach people who might not naturally come through the studio doors. We began running classes out in the community; for teachers and students in schools and colleges, and for various charities including MIND, Midland Mencap and Age Concern. Then, in 2014 we formally partnered with Birmingham Carers Hub to provide unpaid family carers free access to yoga and wellbeing services here at the Studio and at other venues around the City.

For the last 10 years we've helped carers recognise and appreciate the huge role they play in our community and wider society. They devote their lives to others. They are pure *yoga in action.* We, the staff and teachers, are privileged to learn so much from them. Their selflessness, resilience, discipline and commitment to caring for others - with no expectation of anything in return - is yoga! We are simply their guides. We offer carers daily free yoga classes with movement, breathing techniques, mindfulness and meditation so that they have the time and space to witness this. For many it's a vital hour of self-care to relax and replenish, to re-fill their own cup so that they can continue caring. Carers attend classes just like anyone else with a Studio membership, and there's also the option to join online via Zoom.

510 carers have attended our one-off wellbeing and social events around the city

At other times carers love to meet up in a more structured setting, in sessions designed especially for family carers. Our *Carer Life Spa* project is a monthly event to share stories, swap tips, move, stretch, laugh, cry, enjoy a massage, and eat together. The project grew out of Covid times when many services for carers were closed, leaving little opportunity for respite. So, we started a regular online session with a gentle yoga facilitated by the fantastic Kam Bola; life-coach, yoga teacher, and a carer herself. We were bowled over with the feedback we received on the difference these sessions were making, and as soon as social distancing was lifted, we began meeting in person at the Studio. The possibility of joining the event online is still available.

The benefits of a regular yoga practice are now widely known and understood; reduced stress, anxiety and backpain, improved confidence, sleep, eating habits, mobility and flexibility, to name but a few. What the ancient yogis knew thousands of years ago is now backed up by modern science and MRI scanners. The stories that follow, all in the carers' own words, bring these benefits to life, illustrating how yoga has the power to transform lives.

The *Carer Life Spa* project started with yoga and meditation but has also included line dancing, jewellry making, Christmas wreath-making, poetry, creative writing, and hotel spa days. Later this year we're joining forces with THRIVE, the awesome gardening charity to get our hands dirty in nature and practise yoga outside.

The work we do with carers at *Barefoot* has been a catalyst for social networks outside of the Studio; Whatsapp groups, meals out, new friendships blossoming. Some carers have been so inspired by the power of yoga they've gone on to train as Yoga Teachers themselves. We've seen confidence levels soar and whole new worlds opening. All from 'just being bendy'. As the inspirational teacher, Judith Lasater (now in her 80's, so she knows a thing or two), says, "Yoga's not about touching your toes, it's what you learn on the way down".

Faye Fenton, Founder of *Barefoot Birmingham*

"My mood is always boosted by a session, and I feel more relaxed to cope. It is lovely, I feel welcomed into the Zoom class even though I am not in the studio"

M Thain

ANNA & ROSE

"My husband will say "I can't believe you told your mum that" and I say, "it's ok, she'll forget by the morning."

My name is Anna, and I have been caring for my mum, Rose, who has vascular dementia, for the past 4 years, since her diagnosis. I previously cared for my father, who had frontal lobe dementia. His short and long-term memory were fine, it was his decision making that was affected, for example, attempting to crazy pave at 90yrs old during a blistering heatwave.

Unfortunately, we lost him three and a half years ago, due to an aggressive brain tumor. Sadly, he never had the opportunity of moving to their new flat that had been purchased in Harborne.

During my grief and only 8 weeks after his passing, I had to relocate my mum to her new flat, emptying the only home that we ever knew as a family, packing up my dad's belongings and saying farewell to my dad's beloved garden that he had worked so hard on, creating a beautiful calming oasis.

Since then, I have been on autopilot, settling mum into her new life, finding social events for her to attend, and making her feel as comfortable as possible in her new life. I am grateful that mum has been stoic in her approach to her next chapter, sometimes too stoic, as it feels as if I am grieving on my own, with no one to share my pain.

The fact that I was already broken before taking on the role of caring for mum has had a massive impact on my mental health.

I don't sit in a corner and cry, but I am nowhere near the person I was previously. I don't have that thirst for life anymore and I have lost my hyper-active tendencies, in fact now I'm quite the opposite.

I feel as if I don't have the energy to look after mum and fix myself, so I just look after mum. I am fortunate that mum's dementia is in its early stages, and I am trying to maintain her independence for as long as possible, for the sake of ensuring that she is using her brain.

My mum lives around the corner from me and I encourage her to get out of her flat as much as possible, so she regularly comes to mine for a coffee or meal or goes to local coffee mornings at the local churches. I am thankful that my mum is easy going (these days) and is pretty laid back, she'll say yes to whatever I suggest to her.

I consider myself to be mum's personal assistant / talking clock.

"Mum, you're meeting your sister for lunch, you need to leave now."

I call her on average 8-10 times a day, if she's not with me. I'll wake her in the morning, if she's slept through her alarm, advising her what coffee morning she's going to that day and what she needs to do. That's followed up with umpteen other calls to keep her on track.

I have installed a camera in her lounge, so I'll know if she hasn't gotten up and fallen back to sleep. I now realise that before the camera was installed, she fobbed me off, telling me what she thought I wanted to hear. Now, I can keep a watchful eye on her, without calling her when she's busy in the bathroom with her stoma.

I spend a great deal of time preoccupied with mum's daily routine, reminding her to eat and drink at every mealtime on every day.

From the outside, I'm sure it doesn't sound particularly stressful, but it's the little things that stress you out, and they build up after time.

I know some carers who look after their parents feel like they are not heard by their mother or father. It's fair to say I'm stubborn and mum knows that I'll persist until she's done what I've asked of her. I had 20 years of stand-offs with my father (too intelligent and too stubborn for his own good, who still thought he was a puppy at 90).

"No dad, you're 90! I'm going up the ladders, not you!!"

Even though he would eventually come around to my way of thinking, the tug of war was mentally exhausting. I could not bear or cope with the thought of going through that with another parent, so I nipped it in the bud with mum.

When I call the day centre that she attends once a week, and they tell me that she's not accepting their suggestion to drink from her water bottle that she's brought along with her (on my instruction) I ask them to use my name in vain and to tell her that her daughter is going to rip her head off is she doesn't drink it all!

"This is our time where we can just say we're dedicating this time, our energy, for us to put back into what's took out."

anonymous feedback from evaluation of the Forward Carers Small Grants Project, July 2022

NB: My mum has a stoma and it's essential she drinks at least 2 litres of water a day.

On the two days that mum has no diary dates, I don't call her because I'm mentally worn out, I keep an eye on the camera, so I know she's ok, but I need that time to switch off a little and be me for a short while. Then I feel guilty, because it feels nice to not have your head filled with "What do I need to remind her now" and "Has she ...?"

You may think it may be easier to just do it for her, but after going into convalescence for 6 weeks after having her large intestines removed at 80 years old (due to Crohn's Disease), she became quite accustomed to doing absolutely nothing when she returned home, she was happy for my 89-year-old father to do absolutely everything.

So, it is important to me that she does as much as she can for herself whilst she still has the capability to do so.

If I were to give any advice, I would say to invest in technology. I bought mum an Alexa Show, which enables family members to Facetime her. Facial recognition is so important, plus she now uses Alexa to ask what day it is and what the weather forecast is and to set alarms to wake her up from daily naps. I also post diary reminders that visually pop up "Brush your teeth and go to bed, it's 21.30."

The camera has also been a great help, if I can't see her handbag on the lounge door handle, I know that she's gone out.

I bought a label maker and have placed stickers on every

drawer and cupboard in every room, so she knows where to find everything. That's been very useful. I've used it to print reminders for mum, but whether she reads them is another matter!

Dementia Connect, Forward Carers, and Dementia Connect Count are fantastic organisations that can advise carers on what services are available to them and how to access them.

I think it is so much harder to be a carer for a family member, as there are no boundaries, and possibly less tolerance held by the carer.

I am now in the position of relocating my mum's sister over to Harborne, in preparation for the next chapter of her life. She has undiagnosed dementia, and once settled into her new flat, I will be working with adult social services to ensure that she has all the care necessities that she needs.

If you were to know me post 4 years ago and you were to see me now, you probably wouldn't notice anything different about me; I'm still a little eccentric, sometimes funny and generally the one who's goofing around. It's not a façade, it's genuinely how I'm feeling at that time, it's behind closed doors that it becomes most noticeable.

It's true what they say, actions do speak louder than words. I don't harp on about my feelings, (well, at least I hope not). It's the fact that, when I don't have to, I go to my safe space, my bed. To be more productive, I ensure that any appointments that I make are early morning, to kick myself out of bed!

I know that I am carrying emotional baggage that needs

unpacking, and I have planned to receive counselling, I just haven't got round to making an appointment. Maybe I should put it in mum's diary to remind me.

I'm truly grateful to my husband for being so understanding and for being my rock, and for not kicking me out of bed when he knows it's time to get up. He's seen the other side of me, the 'normal' side, and he knows I'm going through something bigger than I've ever dealt with before.

I am writing this after a morning with Kam & PJ at the Halloween Carers Yoga session at *Barefoot Birmingham*, and I felt compelled to put pen to paper, so to speak. I hadn't slept well the previous night and had woken really early, so by the time I had to get up, I was almost falling back to sleep.

The knowledge that I would see my now friends there, and enjoy one of Kam's restoring yoga sessions, was enough to kick myself out of bed. The community and friends that I have made at *Barefoot Birmingham Yoga* over the past few years is so nourishing to me, and every time I go, I feel refreshed, calmer and lighter. I am so grateful for the classes made available to me as a registered family carer.

The stories that we share with one another have made me realise that one carer's experience is typically not the same as someone else's, there may be common traits, but each story has its own unique tale. It is humbling to hear of the uphill struggles that other carers endure, and it makes me appreciate the level of independence that I currently have.

I am also grateful that my husband loves my mum and her crazy eccentric traits. I love the fact that her humour is crass, she loves Ted, the cartoon film, not the conference talks! I love the fact that she enjoys sipping an espresso martini with us in the garden. I love the fact that I can be completely honest with her, tell her about some of my, now once in a blue moon, crazy nights out (think Hangover the movie), and she doesn't even bat an eyelid, but merely laughs. Typically, my husband will say "I can't believe you told your mum that" and I say, "it's ok, she'll forget by the morning."

LIZ & SUSANNAH

"Yoga helps me by providing stress relief and balance in my day to day routines. Without it there would be a hole in my life."

My name is Liz Powell, and I care for my sister Susannah who is disabled with Spinal Muscular Atrophy. In September 2022, Susannah called me sounding very upset as her husband, Steve, had been blue lighted to hospital with suspected sepsis. Steve was Susannah's carer as well as best friend and husband and worked full time as a Project Manager in a major financial institution. I immediately left my home in London and drove to Birmingham where they lived.

Steve ended up being in hospital for 3 months with this serious disease and has had to have amputations of his fingers and thumbs and more recently, below knee. Overnight he went from being a fit and healthy man to being disabled with many challenges ahead.

I decided to relocate to Birmingham so that I could care for Susannah while Steve was in hospital and then help Steve too through his recovery at home. We have a long road to travel until Steve can go back to helping Susannah again and live independently himself, but we remain positive as a team. Each day I help Susannah with washing and dressing, helping her via a hoist into her wheelchair and then vice versa in the evening. I also do the usual activities involved in running a home such as cleaning, washing, cooking etc. Steve has carers 4 times a day to help him, and I include his washing with ours and cook for him. I also take him to appointments and administer his medication. Our days fly by with so many visitors to the house and there are never enough hours in the day.

This change in my life has been a huge adjustment for me as well as them. At times I feel overwhelmed especially as I have led a very independent life and don't have children. I miss my life in London, especially my friends, however it's nice to be close to my family in Birmingham and there is a lovely community spirit in Bourneville where we live. Susannah and I have always been very close, and she is my best friend as well as my sister, so I am never lonely.

Yoga at *Barefoot Birmingham* has had a huge impact on my life in both my physical and mental wellbeing. Yoga helps me by providing stress relief and balance in my day to day routines. Without it there would be a hole in my life. The classes give me time to focus on myself and allow me to switch off completely whilst improving my flexibility and strength. It helps me emotionally to know that the rest of the class understand the challenges when caring for someone who you love unconditionally, and that you are not alone.

It can be very frustrating as people seem to see a happy home where we are all coping, but the reality is very different. This experience has been life changing and at times I feel so sad and emotional and almost numb with everything that has happened. I also get tired with very full-on days. The outside world sees me as always coping and doesn't understand just what is involved with caring for someone both physically and emotionally. Whilst everyone offers to help it's often more of a hindrance arranging this.

To keep myself well I take Molly our dog for a walk every day; being in nature really helps my mind to rebalance. I also play tennis a couple of times a week and the best medicine of all is yoga. All these activities give me time to myself as well as keeping me fit and healthy. I also go to London to see my friends once a month where possible and managed a long weekend in Devon in September. I would advise anyone who is a carer to ensure they allow time for themselves and to have some of their own life too, not just living as a carer. One of the biggest challenges now is taking a holiday, not just a weekend. It's difficult to arrange more than a weekend of friends/family staying and I worry when I am away from Susannah. I try to remember this will not be forever and when Steve has his prosthetic legs, he will be able to help with Susannah. I also focus on all the positives in life and am grateful for something every day. Again, this is something I would encourage all carers to try to do.

Being a carer can be very fulfilling when you see the difference you are making to someone's life. To me it's about living life *with* someone needing help, not living *for* them. Doing things together, having fun together and enjoying each other's company. It's also important to laugh and not take life too seriously. Remember why you are a carer, that there is support out there if you need it via social services and never forget the difference you are making. Try not to worry about the future, you can't change it so live in the present.

"This space is so valuable for us. It validates the struggle we're going through. And yes, it is rewarding, and we do it because we care, but it's having that down time."

anonymous feedback from evaluation of the Forward Carers Small Grants Project, July 2022

TRISH & RACHEL

"My greatest worry is who will care for my daughter when I am no longer able to."

My name is Trish. I am 66 years old.

I care for my 32-year-old daughter, Rachel, and have previously cared for my mum and my dad who both went through dementia.

All my life I have enjoyed keeping busy, I started part-time work at the age of 14, doing various jobs that I enjoyed whilst still in education. Then at the age of 19 I began full time employment, even having two jobs on the go at times.

My much longed-for daughter came along when I was 34, she was born very premature at 26 weeks. She had a very bumpy ride during the months she spent in the Neo-Natal Unit.

I was told that she had suffered irreversible brain damage and would develop Cerebral Palsy (due to lack of oxygen to the brain). I was given a booklet about Cerebral Palsy (I had never heard of it before), the book showed positive images, so me being me just thought OH it won't be too bad, we can do this... my daughter looked active and perfect, just very small! No one was able to tell me how badly she may be affected. It was just a wait and see scenario dependent upon her developmental milestones.

She came home and I just waited and willed her on for the milestones to happen, they did not happen, she did not feed well, she did not sit unsupported, she pulled herself across the floor instead of crawling, she was unable to kneel or stand, she did not use any vocabulary.

I was very lucky to find an inclusive child-minding nursery that cared for my daughter when I returned to work after extended maternity leave. I was determined that we would have the same rights as anyone else to childcare with my daughter. She started at the local special school at the age of 3.

I then decided that I would follow up on my ambition to be a foster carer, I did this for 9 years and we had a lot of fun to begin with, then it became much too demanding. I was also feeling a real need to go back into work, I needed to do something for me and have a space for myself. I found a wonderful term-time only job which I thoroughly enjoyed for 20 years; again, I was determined to find and push for inclusive after-school care for my daughter.

It has been hard caring for a child who is now an adult with severe physical and learning difficulties. A child is much easier to manage physically, now that she is rather large it's quite a physical toll on me as everything involves some form of moving and handling on my part

She must have all her needs met by another person as she is not able to do anything for herself. She has some single vocabulary, and our conversations are very repetitive. She has a very sharp eye and prompts me if I have left something in the wrong place or missed something.

She developed Epilepsy in her teens and Type 2 Diabetes a few years ago, I was very dismayed as I felt that she has more than enough to put up with.

I get up at 6.30am every morning apart from on a Sunday. The carer's arrive around 7am to wash and dress Rachel Monday to Saturday (two of the original carers have been coming to us for 15 years!).

I then add the finishing touches, feed her breakfast and give her medication, brush her teeth and hair. Then we set off to the Day Centre at 10.30am. Since I have retired, I cannot seem to get out of the house much before this, I used to have to leave at 8.15am to drop her off then get to work for 9am. I then have a few hours to myself before I collect her at 3.00pm. I mostly use this time to socialise, meet friends, family, or go to Carer's Groups. I never had much of an opportunity to meet up with people whilst I was working, and I do not go out in the evenings as I am needed at home.

The Carers then return around 4pm to freshen Rachel up and put her PJ's on. When they leave, I generally have to correct her position in the wheelchair and do silly things like pulling her top down at the back of her. I later feed her dinner and her medication, we watch TV, read a book and I hoist her to bed at night. A few nights a week I have to go into her room and see her through her epileptic seizures, sometimes this can be up to 3 times a night.

Unfortunately, Rachel cannot use her hands effectively enough to manipulate objects to help keep her occupied or stimulated, so she needs someone to help her with "hand over hand", otherwise she can only sit and watch what is going on around her.

She loves going outside for a walk as this is quite visual, and she can hear lots of different sounds. I hate it when she is sat in front of a TV for hours. I take her out as much as I can, but I find it a real effort for me nowadays and I am guilty of not taking her out and about as much as she and I would like. We have always had a lot of fun together as Rachel is playful and cheeky, we are very close and have a strong bond.

I have naturally adapted to being a carer as this is a big part of who I am, I care for people, I have a 'mothering' nature. If someone in my family needs help/care I do my best to help them as I did with my parents, despite Rachel's needs, going to work, looking after my home and my husband (Rachel's stepfather) ...I always try and find a way.

I have always been independent and never really asked for help, but I will always try to use resources available to me. When Rachel was a child, we had 10 hours free sitting service per week which I used to go to keep-fit classes or pop out to an appointment. We would use the Family Fund grant to go on a caravan holiday. She went to Respite for a couple of nights every few months.

I married at the age of 47 to a wonderful man who had grown up with a brother with severe Autism. He was well used to the world of caring for someone with a disability, his mom and I got on very well, sharing stories and experiences. I am still very independent and insist on managing things myself as I see Rachel as my 'responsibility'.

"There's a camaraderie – you see friends, or you make new friends. The instructor, Kam is just amazing. As a carer, when she says things, you can feel it – there's such an affinity there, you can feel it."

anonymous feedback from evaluation of the Forward Carers Small Grants Project, July 2022

Thirty-two years of caring has taken its toll emotionally, mentally and physically... My body is ageing, and my joints are troublesome, mentally I am becoming very forgetful and easily flustered, I don't have the energy to fight her corner as well as I used to... anxiety has always been a big issue with caring for her, as her wellbeing, safety and comfort is a constant worry to me.

A year ago, I had to go into hospital for a hip replacement, I had to carefully and meticulously organise how I was going to get through this. I have to say that the Hospital Administration staff worked well with me to offer me an admission date for the week I had arranged for Rachel's respite date. The carers came in four times a day when Rachel came home. People who know me see me as being capable, caring, dependable, easy-going, resourceful and pleasant.

I am relatively introverted and do not do well in conversations, I tend to listen more than I talk. I get anxious when I have to deal with tricky situations. I have to dig deep to deal with challenges. Inside I am very sad and feel low most of the time... I hide my pain by being pleasant and smile a lot.

I suffer with S.A.D during the winter months, I am at my best during the lighter months. Being a carer has made me a stronger person; it is quite a responsibility getting things right for the person you care for. No-one really knows how their life is going to turn out as the unexpected can happen to anyone at any time.

I would have preferred this not to have happened to myself and my daughter, but our life must be lived and appreciated. She brings me great joy in many ways with her personality, I marvel at her endurance and tolerance; I often think that it cannot be comfortable sitting in one position in a wheelchair all day.

I enjoy going to a women-only gym, and also to carers groups for the activities and to socialise. I feel comfortable around the people who attend; I regard it as my 'safe place'. I have enjoyed the carers wellbeing sessions, and I have also thought about taking part online, but I like the company and interaction with other carers. The environment and the ambience are a real treat, and I feel very privileged to have been able to take part. The sessions help with managing stress and give time for carers to take some mental time out and put their caring duties on hold for a short while. I recently did a Mental Health Wellbeing Course which was very useful.

My greatest worry is "who will care" for my daughter when I am no longer able to. I have made an all "about me" folder, outlining all the details of Rachel's care and needs that can be passed on and hopefully be useful when the time comes when I am no longer able to care for her. I am putting a folder together of care homes that I am exploring for the future. Her future weighs heavily on me, it is my biggest anxiety.

I am very happy and grateful to see so much external support for carers, there is a lot of information to tap into online and through carers groups. Life is limiting for carers and their dependents; there are still many areas that are not easy to access. I cannot just put my coat on and go off for a walk or do whatever I fancy whenever I like. We are all very different and have different levels of care, we will care in different ways, some people will enjoy getting together in groups and others are not joiner-inners.

Some carers will have external support from family/friends, some will not. Each carer will find their own way to cope and manage.

Things that have helped me to care

Flexible working
Being organised
Being clear about our needs
Being calmly insistent
Keeping fit - physically and mentally
Keep moving - walking when I have an opportunity
Carers Groups
Well-being activities
Mindfulness
Tapping into resources on offer - they are there for me/us
Carer's Wellbeing Fund - this pays for some of my activities

“I did feel quite alone because I was new to it until I heard about this carers’ pass. The yoga lessons I get to come to, make you feel like someone’s caring for you, someone’s looking out for you. Because it can feel like it’s just me on my own.”

anonymous feedback from evaluation of the Forward Carers Small Grants Project, July 2022

KAY'S STORY

"I have slowed down and learned so much from her. I now do yoga three times a week and am teaching D how to live in gratitude and I am learning myself."

My name is Kay. I am 41 years old and come from a sibling group of 4 myself. I have dreamed of having children and am a caring person and love my siblings. My first experience of caring for a child was that of when my niece was born, I was 21 and she was born at 26 weeks. I took a year out from university to care for her and loved it. She had some health challenges, being premature, but battled through. This experience made me so excited to one day have children of my own.

To further pursue my passion to care for others I decided to retrain from HR to become a social worker. I was eager and keen to progress in my career and felt that I had a lot to give. I got married in 2009 and I qualified as a social worker in 2010. I fell pregnant with my daughter in 2011, I was so happy as my dreams were coming true.

I had a lovely pregnancy, and she was born in March 2012, 10 days over my due date. Our first few moments together were the best experience I have ever had in my life to this day. She was born in water, and I pulled her up towards me and she didn't cry, and we just gazed at one another for 30 minutes. I tried to breastfeed D, and she wouldn't feed. Everyone reassured me that it was normal and not to worry about it. I went home the next day, and D was still not feeding so the midwife came out and said not to worry about it and tried to mix from bottle to breast. D would not have a bottle at all and would scream like I have never heard before. D would not like to be held close and just cried all the time. Day three there were crystals in her nappy, and I took her to accident and emergency. I was told that D was dehydrated.

At this point I felt like a failure; I couldn't even look after my own child. I persisted with feeding her only when she was asleep as when she was awake, she would not allow me to be close to her and just cry. I continued to get support from midwives, health visitors and GP. D lost weight and then put on a little and then lost it again. She was completely breastfed and only during her sleep. So, I would not have visitors and turn the doorbell off so D would not be interrupted, because that would mean that D would not eat and then lose weight.

5 months passed and it was clear that things were not right, D was seen by a pediatrician when she was 5 months old, who described her as multifaceted. The pediatrician did several tests like barium swallow. This was traumatic as she was under general anesthetic. D was referred to a dietitian and sleep counselling. The pediatrician then referred her to the community development team.

D would not settle into a nursery so we would pay for the whole day. I would have to pick her up after 3 hours because she would not eat or drink. Due to this I took another year unpaid from work to care for her. I eventually went back to work for 2.5 days, and this was so tough, I felt like she suffered during the time I was not caring for her. I breastfed her in her sleep for 3.5 years and she did not eat solid foods until she was 4 years old.

D has feeding difficulties, hypersensitivity in her mouth, hypermobility, sensory difficulties, sleep difficulties, struggles to know when she is tired, hungry, hot or cold, and to understand social cues.

Since having D I have changed as a person and no longer prioritse myself. I was sleep deprived and could not have social gatherings as often as I liked or needed as this was not right for D. I felt worried and guilty for the way I was caring for her, I would always question myself and always wanted to do better. Family relationships were strained, and I was blamed for pandering to her, even by my husband. I felt quite alone and disengaged with friends and family.

In 2018 my father passed away suddenly, and I was broken, he was my rock, and he made me believe that I could always carry on. My relationship with my husband was strained and he left the family home. The impact of him leaving on my daughter was detrimental, she lost 5 kilos in 6 weeks and did not sleep.

This was the start of me having my own health issues, I caught covid in 2019 and was very unwell. This scared D and she would get angry at me for resting. This time created anxiety in me and D. I was scared to rest in case she got worried, and it became a vicious cycle.

D was referred for the ASD assessment and this took three years to get an appointment. D had the assessment in 2021, and I received the report in April 2021 to say that she has ASD. This was a difficult time for me, a sense of relief that all that she has experienced was true. Then, with a feeling of overwhelming loss and worry that she won't experience life like everyone else, following with empathy for her struggling herself with things.

D is now 12 years old, and I can say that she is my biggest blessing and now embraces all her differences. I regret spending the first part of her life fixing her and relying on doctors and medicine. My life now is about providing an environment that supports D's sensory needs. I have slowed down and learned so much from her. I now do yoga three times a week and am teaching D how to live in gratitude and I am learning myself.

When we have our difficult days, it can still take a toll on my health. I will continue to appreciate and love D unconditionally. Since accepting the difficulties D has, I can better support her to work through these and help her understand herself.

I have joined the *Barefoot Yoga* carers group and a charity called ATHAC, this has been life changing, connecting with other carers who face the same challenges in life.

be happy. be healthy. be barefoot

JO & SHOLAH

"We connect with lots of carers during our monthly session and have frank and meaningful conversations about how much pressure carers are under. It allows us to fill up our cup."

My name is Joanne Fletcher, I care for my daughter Sholah who is 26 now. I've cared for her from the moment she was born, just as a mother does. But it soon became clear that this tiny being needed extra care. She was born at 37 weeks, weighing 6lb 11, during a normal labour. But within 24 hours of birth, she went blue, stopped breathing and was stiff. She was rushed to Special Care, where these episodes continued. She was diagnosed with epilepsy, we also found out her left kidney wasn't functioning, and her left eye wasn't receiving light into the retina.

For a new mum, hormones raging, it felt like I'd been hit by a bus. I didn't know what to tell people; if I didn't have answers, what could I say? Was it something I'd done during pregnancy, was it something I'd eaten? All these questions flooding my mind. I blamed myself. I had 2 older girls with no problems, so what went wrong?

She was allowed home after 2 weeks, not before we had to learn baby resuscitation. She had an apnea monitor on 24 hours a day, and when she stopped breathing the alarm would go off. We lived on a knife edge. I didn't want to take her out, I had to give up my job and the endless hospital appointments were relentless.

As 6 months turned to 1 year, 2 years, 5 years she never met any of her milestones. She never walked, talked or socialised with her sister.

I felt like I was in a dark place. This was my life, but I never asked for this. I was mourning for a child that was still here. Mourning for my child to hug me, to tell me they love me, walking to school holding hands and talking. What would her voice sound like? What would be her favourite food? How academic would she be? What music would she like? Would she have gotten married? Would she want children? All these taken away from me as her mum.

At 26 she relies on me and her dad for all her needs, feeding, changing, washing, medication, taking her out. But she is a happy, smiley, giggling girl. She loves going to the day centre and socialising with everyone there. It took me years to come to terms with my life, but you have to make the most of it for you. Look after yourself, do things that make you happy, get outdoors. If your cup is filled, then you have the energy and mental clarity to care for your loved one.

I started doing yoga at *Barefoot Birmingham* as my release. It moved my body and helped my mind. The service they provide for carers is amazing. The way Kam talks makes you realise your caring role and helps lift your mental wellbeing, as well as moving your body to maintain flexibility. During Covid we did it on online and it was the only thing that made me feel whole again. We connect with lots of carers during our monthly session and have frank and meaningful conversations about how much pressure carers are under. It allows us to fill up our cup. I for one would be totally lost without this service.

In January 2024 I decided to take the *Barefoot Yoga* teacher training course! I passed in July 2024. I hope to give something back to the people I teach.

I do worry about the future as myself and my husband get older. Where will she be looked after? Will they care for her like I do? Will she be happy? Will she miss me and not be able to express it? But for now, we take each day as it comes.

As a carer, if you feel on your own, struggling with the caring role or not taking time for you, just reach out for help. We are not super-humans, even if we think we are. We must prioritise ourselves first, because if we are burnt out, how can we care?

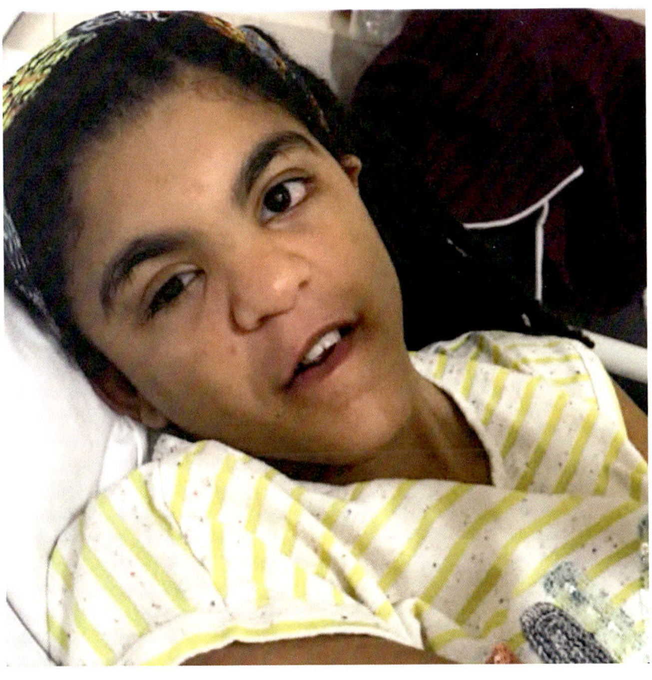

KAM & RAJAN

"For about 11 months Rajan stayed quiet, and his eyes would look at me with deep curiosity, he seemed like a real wise soul."

Rajan came into this world in 2003, he was my second son, and he was tiny in comparison to my first born, 6 pounds 4 versus 8 pounds 12 respectively! As a young mum and maybe feeling more experienced as it was my second, I thought yes, I've got this and was a bit more confident in my role as a new mum, although every experience is different. I was quite laid back, as was Rajan; he hardly moved, he hardly cried, and he slept a lot. I thought maybe I am going to have a generally calm and quiet child. Managing a three-and-a-half-year-old and a newborn, the home already felt quite overwhelming. Rajan didn't feed well, and breastfeeding was a terrible experience for me, as much as I wanted it to be the opposite, it was painful and not at all enjoyable. I'd see mums in the hospital who just made it look like a breeze, and the midwife telling me he'll soon latch on! Well, he didn't, and I felt disappointed but also a slight relief as it was not a pleasant experience.

For about 11 months Rajan stayed quiet, and his eyes would look at me with deep curiosity, he seemed like a real wise soul. He slept well, and didn't complain too much. At one of his appointments just before his first birthday, the pediatrician looked at him and then us, me and my husband, and said that he looked very anemic, and he wasn't reaching milestones that he should have done by 11 months. He instructed us to take him to the Children's

Hospital straight away. After numerous blood tests and finally a bone marrow biopsy the consultant told us he had sideroblastic anemia. I mean at first it didn't really register, and we were both clueless. Then we did what they told us not to do, as soon as we got home, we jumped on the internet and filled our minds with all sorts of information as if by knowing all this we would be able to find a solution. We didn't tell anyone anything for a while, we celebrated his first birthday with family, and they all kept saying how fair skinned and delicate looking he was.

After a few months of diagnosis and being in and out of hospital for further tests and consultation, we were told that the treatment for the condition was a blood transfusion. Not just one transfusion and he will be fixed, but one transfusion every month for the rest of his life! Well after that I felt the floor beneath me break!

Navigating life knowing that you have brought a life into this world and then not knowing how to help is debilitating. I went through several scenarios over and over in my head for years, to be honest 21 years later I still do. Sometimes I don't even know how we have come this far. Rajan has had 240 transfusions to date, his condition means that his red blood cells do not circulate and lie dormant, therefore every four weeks he is given red blood cells that allow his body to function.

I am so very grateful to blood donors, I am so very grateful for the NHS, I am so very grateful to God because Rajan is still here. How did I cope? I have always been an optimist and in this situation, it has served me well, but that doesn't mean I haven't been stressed, because I have.

I can't pinpoint when exactly, but there was something inside of me that jolted one day and I said to myself I can sink, or I can swim. If I sink, I know that the house won't function and I don't like to say it but the fact that I was consumed with dread, worry and in fight mode, my marriage did end up suffering. It wasn't a priority; my priority is my son. The end! That's what I decided. I slowly started to build a daily routine, we needed a sense of security, especially for my eldest son. I wanted to ensure he wasn't neglected, like I had neglected my husband. I thought if I start by taking very small steps, I can create a space that gives us focus, as we were all disjointed.

So, what did I do, you may be wondering? Well, again I can't pinpoint exactly when, but I had a family calendar in the kitchen, and started by putting in Rajan's appointment dates, every month I knew we had to visit the Children's Hospital as mandatory. As a consequence of the blood transfusions there came a host of side effects, iron overload in the liver and heart, 2 MRI scans a year, a hearing test, because in some instances it has been known to cause hearing problems, bone scans as bone density can be weakened. The condition that Rajan has is so rare that there are only 1 set of twins in the UK who have the same, we've never connected with them or found out who they are. This knowledge gave me some hope and that there is a treatment that can help us manage Rajan's health.

The funny thing is, as an outsider looking in you may not even realise that this is going on for us, and I can truly say that my husband, my eldest son and I have all been affected by the diagnosis and found our own ways of coping, sometimes together but many a time in solitude. So, believe me if you and your family are experiencing something similar you are not alone.

I stopped going to family events and parties for a good period of time. I used to put myself in situations where there was an expectation to attend an event, it was the most terrible time as Rajan would never settle and I would get funny looks from family members as if it was my fault that he was crying and screaming. He would scratch me, bite me and when he got a little older, as a diagnosis of autism came, he would kick me and push me! Unfortunately, family members couldn't really understand as they were not in my shoes, and I remember after a good few years I turned around and said to my husband that I couldn't do it anymore and the anxiety of going to various events was causing me deep distress. I don't think he was very pleased, but I had to draw a boundary. I was suffering, I recognised this, and if I was suffering then that would mean I wasn't in good shape or form to look after Rajan. So, if you are experiencing this speak up and don't suffer in silence, stop pleasing people; they don't know what you must do!

I practice gratitude every day, and that's by simply recalling in the morning what I am grateful for and saying it aloud to myself. I used to write it down when I journalled and it's something I still do intermittently. When life feels hard, you must find some goodness to remind yourself that it isn't all doom and gloom. When you start recognising the grateful aspects of your life and really appreciate and value people, places, things, situations, it doesn't take away the pain you are feeling but it gives your mindset a shift, it allows you to soften a little.

I also use a physical diary and combination of phone calendar, to make sure I add all appointments, consultations and events. I also use it to ensure I am filling up my own cup, and add my exercise movement sessions in, it's important so it goes in my diary. I have a massage of some sort at least every 6-8 weeks. I walk in nature every week and listen to a podcast. I am fortunate I can do these things. As Rajan has got older, he can be left at home for a few hours, or my husband, who has become quite introverted over the years, is mostly home unless he's away at work which happens every month for at least a week or two at a time, so I am constantly juggling. I have also learned to listen to my body, and as I am going through the menopause my hormones have been playing havoc. This, combined with Rajan's hormones can sometimes feel like fireworks at Diwali!

It is not selfish to look after yourself, so get that right out of your head, you deserve more, you do so much, and you shouldn't feel guilty at all. Carers sacrifice their time and energy through some of the darkest times and regularly maintaining your self-care helps to keep you from insanity.

I love a weekend lie-in and coffee in bed with a book, although lie-ins tend to be until no later than 8:30am as Rajan gets a bit twitchy, so ensuring I enjoy the simple pleasures in life really helps support my wellbeing. Watching a sunrise and a sunset, seeing a rainbow, looking at the stars in the night sky. The magic of the world around you can ease a troubled mind, so I am reminding you that there is always a rainbow after the rain, despite how dark the clouds above you may feel, the sun will shine.

The carer classes at *Barefoot Birmingham* are a lifeline for many in our community; offering not just yoga, but a safe, supportive space where carers can reconnect, heal, and feel seen. These sessions have created a ripple effect of wellbeing, reducing isolation, improving mental health, and fostering a strong sense of belonging among those who often carry invisible burdens. As both a teacher and a carer, I've witnessed the transformative power of this work, not only in others, but in my own life. Without it, we risk losing a deeply needed sanctuary that has become a cornerstone of care and connection for so many.

"If we don't have a mat or all the right equipment, we can still come – there's no barriers and no social pressure."

anonymous feedback from evaluation of the Forward Carers Small Grants Project, July 2022

CALM MIND
STRONG BODY

SARAH & ADRIAN

"I guess people see me as very capable and I suppose I am, most of the time, but that doesn't mean I don't want someone to look after me for a change."

My name is Sarah and I'm a full-time carer for my husband Adrian, who has Primary Progressive Multiple Sclerosis. We are lucky in that for most of our lives we have both been healthy. We did the normal stuff, had jobs, raised a family, enjoyed holidays and family life and had a good circle of friends.

Then in 2011 Adrian started having investigations for symptoms he was having and was diagnosed with MS in 2012. Initially fatigue was his biggest issue so he couldn't continue to work. We are fortunate that he was able to take ill health retirement, so we can manage financially.

Gradually Adrian's symptoms worsened, and his mobility became more affected, and he gave up things such as driving. By 2020 he had deteriorated to the point of using a wheelchair and now has a very nippy electric chair that he uses all the time. As Adrian's mobility declined, my caring increased and our lives became more structured. I find I cope better this way. I'm a planner and a list person, so structure is important to me.

I recently took early retirement from my part time job and this extra time is enabling me to do activities I enjoy. We have a pattern of things that we do in the week, and this is the starting point for our structure.

I'm up first in the morning and enjoy the peace of having breakfast alone whilst watching the birds on my feeder, I love this quiet time at the start of the day. I make Adrian's breakfast and see if he needs help getting up, mostly he can manage to dress himself and get in his chair. I then have to put wraps on his legs to treat his lymphoedema (a symptom of his lack of movement) and get his medication. Once he's had breakfast he rests whilst I potter, I might bake or do the food shopping and I always tidy our bedroom and make the bed, I love the feeling that the bedroom is a sanctuary or comforting space.

Luckily as he can transfer independently, I can leave Adrian for a few hours, and this gives us both independence and time away from each other. He can wash himself at the sink but needs my help in the shower, and as we have a good-sized adapted bathroom, it's not too difficult maneuvering around him, his power chair and the shower chair, I've got pretty good spacial awareness! In the afternoon we will read, listen to the radio or catch up with family via video calls, we quite often both have a nap as we don't have a brilliant night's sleep. We always try and have our evening meal sitting at the table; I like the fact it makes you hold a conversation with each other.

We don't stay up late and usually head to bed around 10pm. We sleep in the same bed, but Adrian has difficulty getting into bed, so needs my help. He can't turn easily in bed so does need some help in the night but usually is able to wait until he hears me get up for the loo. I find it hard to fall asleep and use meditation apps to help me get off. I usually feel like I've had a disturbed night when I wake up the next day, but my sleep tracker often tells a different story.

I love cooking, so we eat well and importantly I've always got cake in the freezer. Adrian has to have his mid-afternoon medication with food, so that's always a good excuse for tea and cake. We spend a lot of time in the house and love a good film or detective series. My garden is my happy place and I'm always planning things I can change and what veg I'll grow. Escaping outside and getting my hands in the soil makes me feel connected to nature and the mindfulness of it pushes any worries away.

We do have trips out and holidays (in the UK) and have a vehicle that's adapted for Adrian's wheelchair. I must admit though I miss the days when Adrian was the driver and I was the navigator but if I don't drive then I don't get out either, so I just get on with it.

We meet up weekly with a group of friends with neuro conditions and I find myself helping them sort out issues with benefits or Motability or getting adaptations etc. They've nicknamed me "Solutions with Sarah". I guess that's part of my personality, I've volunteered since I was a child and enjoy helping others and ensuring they are treated fairly, it's part of who I am and makes me feel good about myself. I'm currently a Carer Ambassador for Birmingham Forward Carers, a role I'm proud to have.

I've also had health challenges and was diagnosed with kidney cancer in 2015. Following surgery, I made a good recovery and am currently living free from cancer. This diagnosis did change my perspective, and I found coming to terms with a cancer diagnosis very hard. I embraced mindfulness and Tai Chi, but it wasn't easy to stop worrying about the future and what would happen to Adrian if I wasn't around and I have to work on this constantly, so that my mind doesn't defeat me.

I have found a good balance of yoga, swimming and Pilates enables me to have the physical and mental strength to cope, and journaling and number puzzles help me too. Writing this story of my caring experience has been very empowering and has helped me focus on the many positives in my life. I've learned that time spent worrying about the future is time wasted, and no amount of worry will change whatever the future holds. So instead, I focus on today or this week or at the most, this month, and that helps me feel on top of things.

I guess people see me as very capable and I suppose I am, most of the time, but that doesn't mean I don't want someone to look after me for a change. I love a day out where someone else has done all the planning and all I have to do is turn up. Although, I've still had to do a lot before I turn up, as leaving Adrian for a whole day takes organising and contingency planning. I've got a good set of friends, but I don't really share a great deal about my caring role with them, partly because when I'm with them I'm enjoying switching off and partly because I think they'll find it boring.

Adrian is very appreciative of everything I do and does tell me this and generally we work well as a team. Occasionally, frustration beats us both and we might snap at each other, but it doesn't last long and after a chance to cool off we get back on track, we haven't got a choice really and there's no point feeling resentment towards each other. Our situation is nobody's fault, it's just how it is.

I sometimes wish we'd done more travelling when we were young and got on with things we thought we'd have chance to do in retirement and it's certainly something I tell my own children to do. Carpe Diem (seize the day) is a great motto to live your life by.

As I'm bringing this to an end, I wonder what I'd say to someone else starting out on this caring journey and I guess one of the most important things would be, be kind to yourself and to live in the moment. I have found a path that I can navigate for both of us. I'm proud of who I am and of the values that make me the person I am. I'm a good carer and I find joy and contentment in what I do. I'm not living the life I planned for retirement but I'm living the life that's mine and was meant to be.

Barefoot Birmingham introduced me to yoga and through that I've found a way to relax and de-stress. I particularly enjoy the monthly Life Spa session and the fact I can join remotely if needed and still be part of the session is a perfect fit with my caring role. Everyone is so welcoming, and Kam's voice soothes away any stresses of the day. It's one of the few offerings for carers that you can attend in person or remotely and if it wasn't available I would really miss how it supports my wellbeing through the gentle physicality and meeting up with other carers. The relaxation at the end makes me feel ready to take on any challenges the day throws at me!

"I go home and think that I will keep practicing that position. And it's like breathing when you've got the kettle turned on. I presume people take away different things, but the learning doesn't just stop when we leave here, and the love doesn't stop, it carries me through the day."

anonymous feedback from evaluation of the Forward Carers Small Grants Project, July 2022

Hannah Reilly

ANNE'S STORY

"Every carer may feel like they are just about keeping their heads above water. Don't suffer in silence."

Hello my name is Anne. Pictured here is our adult daughter, and we also have an adult son living with us. They have siblings who have flown the nest. We are both now retired and carers. I do feel the weight of juggling responsibilities at times. Both children at home have learning disabilities and autism. Our daughter recognises she has difficulties, but our son doesn't. He tries to "fit in" but then can't understand or accept why not.

In the past 8 years I have had two brain operations for a benign tumor. I may also be looking at cyber knife treatment. This has been challenging for myself and family life. On top of this, I have had depression and anxiety most of my life. I am now in my 60s.

On the outside I have always tried to appear cheerful. I used to be more sociable but now do what I can handle.

Highlights to caring for our children, are witnessing their achievements. Both have attained Duke of Edinburgh awards. Our daughter went to Buckingham Palace to collect her gold award! It was a wonderful day. So good to see many other young people managing the same achievement. I will sound biased, but I believe it can be even more challenging for young people with disabilities. You can see in the photo our daughter holding her gold award and being very happy.

There are the obvious challenges to my caring role. I may be tired and not want to listen to my daughter and son talking to me. I may want to isolate.

My faith, prayer and meditation are a comfort and strength. Also, I like to take myself off to a coffee shop with a book. Or meet with other carers at a free yoga morning for carers. This is great to have a calming experience and a chat with others. Caring responsibilities may be varied. It helps to give my head variety and refreshment to take back to my caring role.

To new carers I would bear the above in mind. Try and hold on to an old hobby, time with friends etc. This can help the caring role not become all encompassing.

Every carer may feel like they are just about keeping their heads above water. Don't suffer in silence. It's possible to find a group of other carers or an activity group that will help to lift your load and lighten your responsibilities.

There's so much in the community, thankfully. A recent yoga morning at *Barefoot* for carers was nice, and free! Gentle stretches, relaxation with positive affirmations. The snacks and drinks were a welcome treat too.

I wouldn't be without our autistic children. Nor would I be without my times apart!

Blessings to all carers.

"I'll eat better today because I'm more aware of self-care. I'm not going to go home and eat crap now, I'm going to prepare myself something good that I wouldn't have done on a normal day."

anonymous feedback from evaluation of the Forward Carers Small Grants Project, July 2022

barefoot

ALISON HOPE'S STORY

"No mud, no lotus"

The Māori word for autism is takiwatanga it means, 'in their own time and space'. The word autism, from its Greek roots and in its purest form, is 'aut', meaning self and 'ism' which implies a state of being or condition. A state of being oneself.

Autism. Our Journey.

I was 42 when my second son was born. My joy was such that I told the midwives I would try to have another baby the next year. I almost succeeded, my third son was born 18 months later. So lucky. So happy.

At three years old my second son was diagnosed with autism and moderate learning disabilities.

And then our journey began.

The Start

Our son has a love of words and was asking how to spell random words from a very young age. That is where the porcupine reference comes from in this poem. Plus, it rhymed.

Speech Delayed

Speech delayed, it was said
Do you have trouble getting him to bed?
Does he babble or wave bye bye?
Can he hear? Let's just try.
Is it epilepsy, will we just test?
Honestly, please, just do your best.
Nursery doesn't work for our son
It will get better, try one to one.
Postman Pat on a loop
Bowels full. He hates to poop.
He loves to bounce and climb and run
At times we all have so much fun
He won't turn left only right,
Make sure the car window is shut tight,
Read the same stories time after time
How do you spell porcupine?
Watch Thomas the Tank, again and again
Drinking water from drops of rain
People look and people stare
He doesn't notice. He doesn't care.
Next, it's school, the minibus run
Is he happy, having fun?
At home it's shouts and slamming doors
Banging his head on the wooden floors.
I've just discovered he can read.
Learning new words at such a speed.

Why does knife start with K?
These questions are how we spend our day.
Life with autism is confusing
Sometimes winning, sometimes losing.
I fight to keep the flame of hope alive
That our boy will learn, and grow, and thrive.

Moving On

After a mostly successful time at an autistic specific primary school, apart from a few months of school refusal and minibus issues, our son moved on to an autistic specific secondary school.

Special Events

Having a child with autism changed our lives. Those differences became the norm for us. Whooping down the road, stimming, ear defenders, jumping at bumps and bangs, knowing more about Sponge Bob Square Pants than you ever thought was possible. Special events highlight how different our lives can be.

21st birthday

So, our son was 21 on Sunday. These special dates throw into sharp perspective how different life is for him and us. He had 6 cards; he is glad his birthday is over and relieved to learn that he doesn't have to learn to drive or get married just because he is

21. He was dreading a party or a cake-that might mean people singing happy birthday. He spent his birthday money on DVDs. 21 in total from HMV. Our lad can use the words anthropomorphic, protagonist and antagonist perfectly well in sentences - usually describing Pingu, Pingu's father or all the Simpsons cast. He has perfect pitch and knows lots of words in lots of languages. If he can be bothered and, if given your date of birth, he can tell you the day on which you were born. He doesn't know that these talents are anything special, they are just how it is. He doesn't understand money or people. The world and societal expectations are so difficult for our son. It is as though he is watching life go on around him through a glass window, wanting to be a part of it all, but doesn't have the key to unlock it.

He finds it too confusing. He can go no further in conversation than asking someone how old they are; and he asks them that time and time again. He knows people work in our local pub and they are under his age of 21, he says it is just their personality. He collects videos and DVDs and takes bundles out with him to try and find common ground to make conversation with strangers, conversations where he doesn't have to answer questions, and nothing is expected of him. He runs along the street whooping and stimming and waits for me to go across roads with him. Anxiety awaits him around every corner.

Unique and often misunderstood. He is our son.

Bleak Times

And then comes the move out of children's services. This was something I wrote about three years after we had a placement fail spectacularly. Our son was at home full time and finding suitable provision was proving to be an uphill battle. I came across his school graduation photograph which took me back to that time of hope and fear for his future.

Below summarises what was possibly one of the bleakest times in our journey. We had a couple of care providers withdraw their offers of a place for our son after working with him and us for a while. I sometimes lost hope and was afraid of what his and our future held.

Home

When our children graduated from secondary school three years ago, few of us parents had any idea of what lay ahead for them in the next few years. The last three years for us has been difficult, frustrating, exhausting, and uncertain. In our case a failed placement has meant our lad has been at home with us for most of this time. During this period, I have had to fight to find suitable care. I have found strength and resilience I never knew I had. I have also broken down pushed beyond the limits of my endurance. Through all of this we have our son whose bravery, resilience, and ability to keep trying makes me proud and who I love more and more every day. His behaviours do challenge, his lack of understanding of life and people can and has led to him becoming overwhelmed and losing control. We have had the police at our door, he has banged his head so hard that it has bled. We have also had laughs, our boy is quirky, we find humour in the most unexpected of things. He is a young man and deserves to be treated as such, he has a life but needs support to navigate that life.

He needs to be appreciated for who he is. We need well-funded services that have time to listen to and support families like ours. I wish luck, happiness and hope to all the parents whose children are now embarking on the next chapter of their lives.

Then lockdown and another care provider withdrawal. Our son was eventually at home with us, full time, for five and a half years. Our world was shrinking. He and I went out almost daily. He would only go out with me. I was hyper-vigilant for signs of any potential for him to panic. A dog, a noisy car, babies crying. Sometimes we sailed through these events and sometimes we didn't. Neither of us had a social life apart from each other. It was scary.

The Last Step…I hope

Our son who is now 24, moved into supported living in March 2022. The transition consisted of 10 months of visits and outings with a brilliant care team. He sometimes refused to go out with the team, but they were patient, they were in it for the long haul. In July 2022 I visited him in his new home for the first time since he had moved in. I was excited and nervous to see and hug him.

He has changed. I understand that I am no longer such a big part of his world. He has always compartmentalised his life, he used to find it difficult when we went to his school. He is slimmer and more independent. He made me a cup of tea for the first time ever. He looked into my eyes, and we touched our forehead and noses together. Something we have always done.

What Helped Me Through

Apart from deep and unconditional love, the kindness of strangers, meeting brilliant parents, being introduced to meditation, and attending lots of training events, millions of things have helped me through the challenging times. Trying to understand the world view of someone with autism is just one of those things.

Unpaid carers are under immense pressure physically and emotionally. Burn out can and does result in physical and emotional breakdown. The opportunity to completely relax in the calm surroundings of *Barefoot Yoga* Harborne is immeasurable. For us to come together once a month, take part in a tailored yoga class, enjoy a shoulder massage and have snacks provided is a way of letting go, cares float away, the ever growing to do list can be put on hold for a short time, we are encouraged to feel that our well-being is important. That we are important. To get back in touch with our bodies. The monthly class is something to look forward to, a haven to chat and share stories, worries and laughs with other carers. Friendships are forged; hugs are plentiful. Thank you to all the team at Barefoot. You allow us to feel joyful and strong.

Books

Information I found when our son was first diagnosed tended to be negative and didn't give us a lot of cause to hope for a happy future for him. I decided to read books written by people with autism to try to understand what is happening on the inside, not just what is observed on the outside.

The first book I read which was written by someone with autism was, 'Through Alien Eyes' by Jasmine Lee O'Neill. The whole book gave me a deeper understanding of autism, but the words that stay in my heart and memory and have given me hope and positivity about the future for our son are,

'I hope you can celebrate who you are and feel strong in your simplicity and purity. Inside you in a very deep place, can live a universe. You can see yourself as a multi-faceted stained-glass window. Think of your life as bursting with radiating intense moods and colours. Your life can be a rainbow.'

My son doesn't have the self-awareness to think like this. But the beauty of the words affected my whole outlook on autism.

Other books I have read by authors with autism and found helpful albeit a sometimes painful read, are,

Nobody Nowhere by Donna Williams, a sometimes-disturbing book about a young woman who was misunderstood and unable to understand herself until she heard the term autism at the age of 25. An Australian author born in 1963 she is also a talented artist. She has written follow up books, notably ***Somebody, Somewhere.***

Martian in The Playground by Claire Sainsbury. A high functioning autistic young person's view of life in a mainstream school.

The Reason I Jump by Naoki Higashida translated by David Mitchell. I read this book relatively recently, my son has always loved to bounce and jump. This book helped me to understand that need and so much more.

Documentaries

There are more programmes, reality TV and documentaries that include autism available now than when my son was first diagnosed. I often cannot watch those programmes as I occasionally find them voyeuristic, too simplistic, or just offer a one-dimensional view of autism. Sometimes, they just make me sad.

But a few that I have found interesting and helpful are,

A is for Autism. A short animation, made in 1992 I watched it several times after our son was first diagnosed.

Life Animated. A documentary showing how a young man with autism made sense of life through Disney films. I believe there is now a film based on this original documentary.

The Woman Who Thinks Like a Cow. A Horizon documentary from 2006 features Temple Grandin explaining her life with autism. Not a documentary, but a film which I thought gave a realistic portrayal of an individual with autism.

Snow Cake 2006 with Alan Rickman and Sigourney Weaver. The film does not have autism as it's central theme, but Sigourney Weaver gives an excellent portrayal of a young woman with autism.

Music

Our son didn't really like to have music on in the house unless it was of his choosing. Certain pitches were jarring for him. We jokingly called him the noise police when he would march into a room and switch the radio off.

When I had the opportunity to listen to music two songs that helped and continue to help me to feel strong when I feel weak and cheer me up when I feel sad are:

Unstoppable by Cia the line, 'Leave my sunglasses on while I shed tear', particularly resonates. We are unstoppable.

I Feel Good by James Brown. Just to remind myself that I can feel good even when I feel invisible.

Finally

I never want to minimise how tough life can be for families and carers who have children with autism and/or learning disabilities. Our family has hit some very low times. Throughout, I have tried hard to hold on to the positives. I hope I am a more tolerant, patient, kind, and open hearted, person than I was before our son was born. I no longer worry about a dusty house. I have found out so much about neurological divergence and have learnt to value that difference and not be afraid of it. I have met so many kind and understanding people, who have given me faith in human nature.

Our son is now busy, content and making progress. And whilst we are not taking anything for granted, we hope this is the final step on his road to a fulfilled life which he can carry on with when we are no longer around.

As for me, I am entering the next chapter of my life and look forward to that with hope, trepidation, and curiosity.

14 months on

Our son has now been in supported living for 14 months. We see him on a fortnightly basis. Those dates are sacrosanct, they will be in his memory, and they are in big letters on my calendar.

He is doing well with his care team and his anxiety levels have lowered, he has started to occasionally see us in our local area on every other outing, as he calls our meetings.

He has come to our house a few times, but sadly, this leads to our younger son having bad dreams after the visit. It is still a tight rope. I wrote this after our get together last Monday. I hope it encapsulates how things are now.

Breathe

Tiny feet pitter patter across my chest. In 2,3,4 out 2,3,4,5,6,7,8. Rod Stewart is eating his heart out because of an ill-judged affair with Maggie May.

A sudden lurch. We come to a standstill. In 2,3,4. I glance at the clock, still plenty of time.

Slipping Into first gear we start again, winding through unfamiliar streets, weaving our way around

haphazardly parked cars. Nearly there. A tightening in my stomach. Out 2,3,4,5,6,7,8.

Our destination, Nando's, barely 5 miles from home. I stand in the sun, waiting. Observing the

shoppers go by. The ubiquitous brown paper Primark bags interspersed with colourful bags for life.

Here they are. My heart somersaults. I smile. We hug. He is not wearing his ear defenders.

"Meet back here at about 2.30? Has he had a good week? Great. See you later."

Another hug and a kiss. We link arms.

"Paul O'Grady, aka Lily Savage is deceased. "

"He is."

"You liked him. "

"I did; he was funny."

“He was like Ru Paul. A drag... like you watched with my brother”.

“That’s right, Ru Paul is a drag queen. I used to love watching that with F.”

“Paul O’Grady aka Lily Savage loved dogs more than people.”

“He really did love dogs.”

We make our way into the still quiet restaurant.

Another hug, like butter oozing through the holes of a crumpet my love seeps silently out of every pore. I am so full I feel I am about to explode and when I do it will be glitter, confetti and ribbons catapulting forth from my body.

We hug again. I breathe.

ME & MY DAUGHTER

by Y. M.

"What people see on the outside and what is actually going on for me I don't ever reveal..."

Me, my special daughter and our family. I am the main carer of my special daughter, T. Her dad helps with caring whenever it's needed. We are both retired now and share the caring and have been since her birth. We also have another daughter who is five years older than T, she's 48 years old now and married with two children. We are grandparents to two beautiful teenagers.

T was born prematurely at 26-week gestation and weighed 1kg (a bag of sugar). She was kept in an incubator for 14 weeks with lots of wires and tubes for oxygen and feeding, and a monitor to check her breathing, heartbeat and oxygen level. Our world turned upside down with worrying, stress, anxiety, tiredness and anger - why did it happen to us? We had to care for our first child, who was turning five years old then. It was very hard to juggle, balance and fit in everything with work, appointments, meetings, visiting hospital, picking my daughter up from school, cooking, housework and faith related activities. We had to look into the wellbeing of us all; physically, mentally and socially.

Life was like a rollercoaster at times; it needed navigating and juggling with day-to-day planning. It started from waking up, personal care, structuring the day, prioritising appointments, meetings, events, mealtimes, activities, shopping etc. etc.

T had delayed development and at the age of two was diagnosed with mild cerebral palsy which affected her vision (severe visual impairment, supported by the eye department at Birmingham Children's Hospital), and her mobility (poor balance, supported by physio and occupational therapy).

T's moderate learning difficulties required speech therapy and a neurologist. She attended a special needs nursery, followed by a special needs school and then a special needs college.

T has basic numeracy and literacy skills. She doesn't have any academic achievements. In 1999 she was registered blind with very limited forward vision - no peripheral vision. She was offered support by the Adult Social Care team and had funding for up to five years to attend Queen Alexander Specialist College for adults with sight loss and disabilities. She was a residential student and developed daily living and social skills from 2005 to 2010.

There was no institution available at the end of her funding to help her continue with the skills she had developed to be independent with some support. After lengthy discussions, QAC bought a three-bedroom house near the college to do a pilot project study. T was the first female to live with two other ex-students independently with some support and sleep in staff. The three students enjoyed their independence, the social aspects and activities. The project was called IP (Independence Plus) sheltered house, where the staff supported the three students between 5pm-10pm and then the sleep-in staff came in from 10pm-7am. T was supported and would be ready for 9am and go off to college or to the gym. It was a very positive pilot study and now the College has seven houses nearby which house up to three students, an eighth house is due to open soon too.

T moved into the IP sheltered housing with support in 2011, she shares a 3-bedroom house with 2 other ex-students. She is quite happy there and has the best of both worlds as QAC is quite near to where we live. She enjoys her independence and socializing, as all the residents in the IP scheme share special days, such as birthdays, and they visit each other's houses for birthday parties, they plan to go out and arrange evenings out.

She comes home when she is free at the weekends, for festivals like Eid, and birthdays. The support she has is from 5pm-10pm and then from the sleep-in staff through the night until 9am the following morning. From 9am until 5pm she does her own activities with some support like travelling or walking. We must plan her activities every week to fit in and prioritise appointments, meetings, events, education, secular and religious (lifelong learning).

The impact of being a carer over the years has been up and down, with stress, anxiety and worrying about the future - what will happen and how will she cope?

My own physical, mental and emotional wellbeing has been affected. Physically I was tired, exhausted and had to do a lot to fit in everything. I developed high blood pressure and needed medication for several years. I have asthma and use a pink inhaler daily. I used to need a blue inhaler too, for when I got breathless, and I was using it quite a lot, but since starting the yoga and wellbeing sessions at *Barefoot Birmingham,* I rarely need to use it.

I have arthritis in my wrists, thumbs and knees. I take pain relief to manage the extreme pain I feel at times, but yoga has improved my posture, my breathing, mobility and it has lessened the pain in my knees and wrists. It has changed my life holistically and physically.

Socially getting together with other carers, talking, listening, and learning from each other, means I feel I am not alone in my caring. I feel good and energised to face the challenges.

I attend yoga sessions on Monday, Tai-chi on Tuesday, and I attend the free carers session on the last Thursday of the month at *Barefoot Yoga*. I go swimming with my daughter at the weekend. The rest of the week I do some light exercise and walking. I try to rest and have 'me time' at the weekends after doing house chores.

My faith has given me the strength and courage to cope and do whatever I have to do as a carer and a mum. What people see on the outside and what is going on for me on the inside, I do not reveal, and I keep a mystery.

Initially I had not heard the word "carer". I was T's mum, and I just carried on caring as all mothers do. I did not expect any help or support. I just did my best; I did what I could and hoped it was right.

People sometimes felt sorry for me when they realised how much caring was involved, caring for a very ill and premature baby and caring for a full-term normal baby. It was very challenging for a long time, there was no one I could talk to about how I felt, there was not enough time, ever, to do what I wanted to do, I just had to fit it all in.

Later when I learnt that I was a carer and met other carers I realised I was not alone struggling. There were many other carers in worse situations than me. At carers sessions we listened to each other and learnt a lot from one another - some coping mechanisms, to be patient and to have a positive attitude. Take it slow, one day at a time and don't worry too much about the future.

The highlights for me are attending carer sessions, yoga, tai-chi, going on trips, and attending events with other carers and our cared-for.

Here are a few tips for someone new to caring, someone who may be younger or for someone who may find it hard to talk about their caring responsibilities or could be suffering in silence:

1. Always keep faith with you.
2. Have a positive attitude.
3. Look after your well-being; sleep, nutrition, relaxation and me-time.
4. Have patience; one day at a time and do not worry too much about the future.
5. Have the courage to speak up, be brave and do your best.
6. Talk and listen to other carers - find a carer focused session, do some training.
7. Keep on learning about the condition of the cared-for, and the role of the carer.
8. Attend yoga, tai-chi and mindfulness classes.

"Everytime we come we get a little gift - that to me is something to say, you are someone, you're worth it, thank you for just being here."

anonymous feedback from evaluation of the Forward Carers Small Grants Project, July 2022

SHEVA & RAPH

Sheva-Viv Martin (Viv Manjaro), Mother of Dearly Beloved Raphael Martin-Shervington

"They say that a mother is a son's first Love, and a son a mother's last".

Three Little Days

Raph, I think we've arrived.

This is the spot.

What say you?

"Yes Mumlum, we reach".

"It's kinda like a bigger, bolder brighter version of Grooms Cottage".

For certain.

The main difference is that Holy Mount Kilimanjaro makes the vibrations here so very potent. You can feel it in your skin; in your lungs; as well as through your feet. What a Blessing!

Viv sat eating a thoroughly delicious breakfast; especially enjoyed because someone else had prepared it for her. It was impossible not to notice the multifarious birds frolicking in the hedgerows through the open antiquated windows. Ahhh she thought, Raphael's Friends have come to greet him.

To greet us. Karibu!

Marangu Lodge. Eight and a half acres of serene beauty. But there's company if you seek it. Open spaces, closed space, lush flower beds, lush green lawns. Earth, air, wind and then the mist off Mount Kilimanjaro for water.

The new twin bed apartment to which she was moved to for her second day due to the large booking of 36 people that were arriving to start their climb was many hues of blue and magenta, luckily nearer to the 'chosen spot'.

The mini-carpet bag was repacked with the keepsakes from Maxine, lighter, feathers, crystals and most important Raphs Ashes.

She would wait until high noon when staff were busy preparing for the new arrivals. Smiling at the thought of 'High Noon'; usually associated with Western Shoot-Outs. There'd be no shoot out today just a quiet, private Ceremony.

"They say that a mother is a son's first Love and a son a mother's last".

How true. Would there ever again be such intensity of emotion felt for another.

Intense Love. Pain. Fear. Joy.

This day there is a combination of these intensities but mostly Joy. Because Raph's Presence. Raph's Energy is being keenly experienced.

She stands so tall and proud. Radiating wonderous vibrations to all who are able to feel her potent power.

Raph whispered 'Bless' as he saw with my eyes the near silhouette of Kilimanjaro through the mist in the early hours of the breaking dawn.

Raph and I had climbed the triangle of 3 Holy mountains together at his request for his 25th Birthday. Holdston Down and Yes Tor in Devon and Brown Willy on Bodmin Moor. We didn't quite make it to the top of the last one because the weather was changing and evening was approaching so we just stopped on the side of the mountain, chanted Holy Mantra and Prayed.

I walked tentatively along a secluded path to the 'chosen spot'.

Great, "hey-ho-nobody-at-home".

Raph laughed at my feeble attempt to carry out a ritual swim in the freezing water of the mini pool.

Drying off in the sun I sat smiling as I remembered little Raph with his cousins Tem and Bish at the pool in Mo-bay Jamaica. And how Maxine had saved Raph's life that day when he had jumped into the pool aged one and a half unexpectedly. Then the unforgettable incident at the river Wye when an older Raph swam across the river despite my profuse objections and was pulled under by strong undercurrents and had it not been the passing by of a very capable canoeist who heeded my screams of help and rowed to his aid a pleasant picnic by the river would have ended in tragedy.

No footsteps approaching, the coast is clear.

Time to honour Raph again.

Step one. Sprinkle Raph's Ashes along the chosen spot of wild green grass.

“Ashes to Ashes Dust to Stars”.

Pause. The coast remains clear.

Step two. Place the four crystals separately in well-hidden spaces, hang the keepsakes. I didn’t feel able to part with the two Keepsakes that I had brought with me; the child size ceramic hedgehog which was the first Mother’s Day present that Raph had ever bought me and the child size metallic VW Traveller bus which was the last present that I gave Raph a year before on a visit to Brighton to see his Godmother Teresa.

So, I hung the two talismans that Auntie Maxine had given me on the untamed hedge away from curious eyes.

Still alone

Still quiet. Good

Now to release the feathers along the stream.

I watch them float gently away, well nearly. Some of the feathers clung to the side of the bank refusing to flow downstream. Everything in its own time.

To where does this stream flow I wonder?

Forgetting to be mindful of the time I try to follow the sound of the current. Wandering across some grassland I descend a few deep steps and looked down what I estimated to be at least 1000 feet. It was a wild chasm with gigantic cheese plants and banana trees.

I catch my breath goodness, gracious me; a fall to that riverbed would be certain death, go back.

Grateful that one hour after my arrival for Raph’s Ceremony I have been undisturbed by none of the many guests staying at Marangu Lodge.

Back to the main site I take some video footage, a bit of a mess really but I know Raph will forgive me. He knew this mission on my own was not an easy one.

"Mumlum, you're not alone. Be still. Be quiet. I'm right here."

I relax and sit beside the chosen place. It's true.

You're here.

Birdsong.

I return the next day at noon to meet a beautiful cat sitting under the table.

Hello I say. You've also come to visit Raph.

UNDER ARMOUR

A Compilation of Poems

"...and if you want to come and lie down and enjoy what you can - she just gives you that option, this is a safe space."

anonymous feedback from evaluation of the Forward Carers Small Grants Project, July 2022

LOST

I've lost someone to dance with
I've lost the person I walked up hills with
I've lost the one who swam in the sea with me
I've lost the retirement we planned
I've lost the chance to childmind any grandchildren
I've lost weekends away with the girls
I've lost the chance to leave the driving to you
I've lost someone to put the bins out
I've lost the person who went in the loft
I've lost the chance to cuddle on the sofa
I've lost the person who held the door for me
I've lost someone to empty the dishwasher when I'm tired
I've lost the person that made me a coffee
I've lost the chance to have a bath
I've lost the person that would nip to the shops
I've lost someone to help with the shopping
I've lost long haul holidays
I've lost short haul holidays
I've lost spontaneity
I've lost confidence
I've lost the future
I've lost us
I've lost myself
I've lost out

by Elizabeth Drake

I wrote this in 2011, when our son was 13 in response to an open request from the National Autistic Society for poetry. He was not wearing ear defenders full time when I put this together. He does now. We also used to make stories up together and consequently I had given to me the alter egos of John, Woody (as in woodpecker) and Tweety Pie. A bonus of this is that I have learnt to whistle well.

THOSE NOISES

I look into his wide green eyes,
My boy, my angel, my love
Shut up, he says. That's not kind.
Sorry? Do I need to apologise?
How was school? Don't talk don't ask
Okay my love, my star
Just check the fan, make sure it's off,
Closer, not too far
Those noises, horns and coughs and barks
Put your fingers in my ears
I'm so scared, you might say no,
I'm panting, full of fear
It's okay I won't say no, mom is always here
Be Tweety Pie, be John, be Woody
I whistle, hum and play
Mom's too tired for a story now
It's the end of our long day.
Now he's dancing to a Disney tune.
Jumping, twirling, clapping, shouting with joy,
His face lights up, I smile with him.
My beautiful, autistic boy.

by Alison Hope

MY AUNT

In the quiet hours of the early dawn,
When morning light starts to gently yawn,
I find her there, my dear, frail aunt,
With the heart of a lion, so vibrant but gaunt.
She sits, a beacon of stories untold,
Inquisitive eyes, her spirit bold,
Listening intently to my every word,
Her laughter, a song from a joyous bird.
She asks of my day with endless cheer,
Her questions show she truly cares,
In the symphony of our daily chat,
She finds delight, and I cherish that.
Her fussiness, a charming quirk,
In her world, perfection is the work,
She hums a tune, her favourite song,
In her melody, I find where I belong.

Caring for her is more than a chore,
It's a gift of love, an open door,
To a world of wisdom, laughter, and grace,
In her presence, I've found my place.

by N. N.

DON'T DIE BEFORE ME

Most nights I cry
Most days I feel it... this sixth sense... that you will die
Before me
I try and I try to keep the faith and believe
If I pray and meditate surely, I will receive
I try my best to hold it together
My heart is as delicate as a feather
Most nights I cry
Somedays I feel it... this knowing... that you will die
Before me
I have watched you sleep at night
Crept into your room and tried not to give you a fright
Just to watch you breathe
Please don't leave...
Someday the pain I feel is unbearable
I must live to accept your condition is not repairable
My eyes feel so dry from the tears I cry
This niggling feeling never leaves me... I don't want you to die,
Before me
I put on a brave face, every morning we embrace
We start each day with hope and grace
Life sometimes feels like such a race, but when I look at your shining face
I know I wouldn't want to be in any other place

Anon 2025

Relax your body
Calm your mind
Renew your spirit

GENTLE SELF-CARE & SELF-LOVE TIPS

from Bee of Bee's Holistics

Boglarka or 'Bee' 'is our complementary therapist with the most magic of hands! Bee provides therapeutic massage to help guide carers back to themselves. Mum of two and a big Star Wars fan, Bee's passion lies in creating a safe space for people to feel seen, heard and cared-for.

Always remember that caring for yourself is not selfish, it is what enables you to continue giving to others from a place of wholeness.

Always with love, Bee ✨

- ***Be aware of the beauty in ordinary moments***

- ***Be compassionate with yourself when you make mistakes***

- ***Be willing to set boundaries with others***

- ***Be grateful for the small joys throughout your day***

- ***Be accepting of your emotions without judgment***

- ***Be mindful of your body's needs for rest and nourishment***

- ***Be open to asking for help when you need it***

- ***Be gentle with yourself during tough times***

- ***Be patient with your personal growth journey***

- ***Be connected to what truly matters to you***

Remember that unlike a to-do list where items get checked off, this to-be(e) list represents ongoing intentions for how you want to show up for yourself. There is no "completing" these as tasks - they are practices to return to, repeatedly as part of your self-care journey.

Honour Your Basic Needs

- Nourish your body with foods that energise rather than deplete

- Prioritise sleep as sacred healing time

- Stay hydrated throughout your day

Create Micro-Moments of Peace

- Take three deep breaths before entering a caregiving situation

- Find small pockets of stillness between tasks

- Establish a simple morning ritual that is just for you

Set Loving Boundaries

- Remember that "no" can be a complete sentence

- Recognise when you're approaching emotional depletion

- Ask for specific help from those in your support network

Reconnect with Your Body

- Place your hands on your heart when feeling overwhelmed and breath in and out 'through your heart space' – notice the relief at the end of each exhale

- Release tension through gentle stretching, movement, or self-massage

- Notice where you hold stress and consciously soften those areas

Practice Self-Compassion

- Speak to yourself as you would to a dear friend

- Acknowledge the immense value of your caregiving work

- Allow yourself permission to be imperfect

Find Community

- Connect with other carers who understand your experience

- Share your challenges without judgment

- Celebrate the big and small wins together

Image: Bee, complimentary therapist, with carer Jo, at Winterbourne House & Gardens.

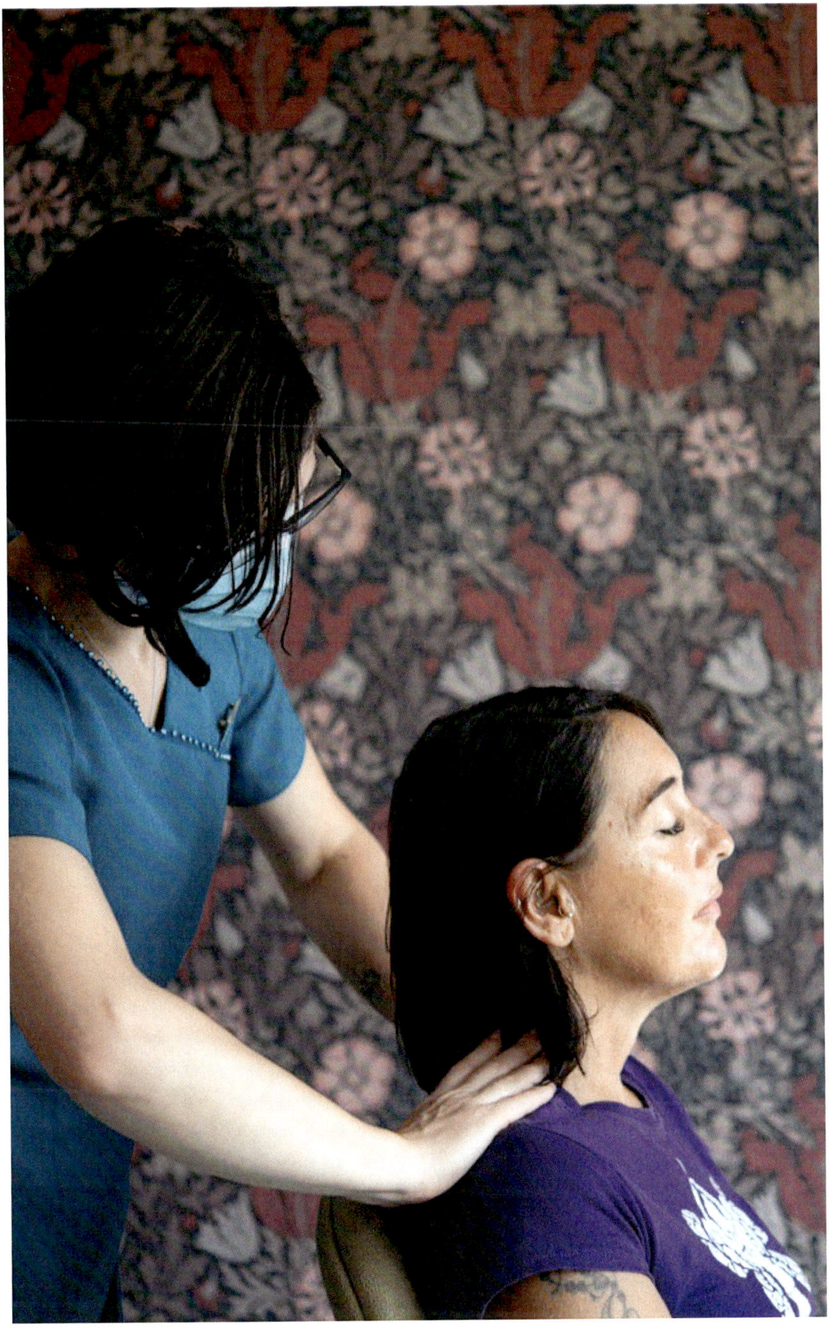

1. I am organ
2. I am forward
I am the best
of carer
am patient
caring
I am deter
am strong
I am loving.
I am Ressoureful
I am Happy

Affirmations

Affirmations are powerful tools that can positively impact your mental and emotional well-being. Here are some key benefits:

1. Reprogramming the subconscious: Affirmations help replace negative thought patterns with positive ones, promoting a healthier mindset.
2. Boosting self-esteem: Regularly practicing affirmations can enhance self-confidence and self-worth.
3. Reducing stress: Positive affirmations can lower stress levels by reducing the production of cortisol, a stress hormone.
4. Improving overall well-being: They can lead to better mental and physical health, including improved resilience and reduced anxiety.
5. Encouraging positive behaviour: By affirming core values, affirmations can motivate productive responses to challenges.

These affirmations can help you stay grounded, motivated and resilient in your caregiving journey. Pick one per day and say it first thing in the morning or write it on a post-it note and place it on the mirror, the fridge, a noticeboard or somewhere you are likely to see it as a visual reminder. You can repeat affirmations daily or whenever you need a boost of positivity and encouragement.

Positivity

I bring light and positivity to those I care for.

My compassion makes a difference every day.

I am a source of strength and support.

I choose to see the good in every situation.

My positive energy uplifts those around me.

Mindfulness

I am present in each moment, fully engaged.

I breathe deeply and find calm within.

I am mindful of my needs and the needs of others.

I embrace each day with a clear and focused mind.

I find peace in the present moment.

Self-Love

I am worthy of love and respect.

I honour my own needs and feelings.

I am proud of the care I provide.

I deserve kindness and compassion from myself.

I am enough, just as I am.

Hope

I hold onto hope even in challenging times.

I believe in the possibility of better days.

My hope inspires those I care for.

I trust that things will improve.

I am a beacon of hope for others.

Faith

I have faith in my abilities as a carer.

I trust the journey and the process.

My faith guides me through difficult moments.

I believe in the power of love and care.

I have faith in the strength of the human spirit.

Self-Care

I prioritise my well-being and self-care.

I take time to rest and recharge.

I nourish my body, mind and soul.

I set healthy boundaries to protect my energy.

I am deserving of care and attention.

I am committed to taking care of myself.

Kam, Faye, Tania and the 'Carer Life Spa' Barefoot Birmingham team, at Forward Carers 10 Year Anniversary celebration in December 2024.